PEAK P[...]

You Ca[...]er!

All royalties of this book go to Mission Nebraska

By Ron Brown & Gordon Thiessen

Copyright 1999 Cross Training Publishing
Published by Cross Training Publishing
P.O. Box 1541
Grand Island, NE 68802
1-800-430-8588
Cover Art by Lynda Lambrecht Stych

PEAK PERFORMANCE

Introduction

Few sports programs have achieved the success of Nebraska football. It has been my pleasure to both play for the Cornhuskers (1975-80) and work closely with the coaching staff on various book projects during the past decade.

Coach Ron Brown's insight into this incredible program will help anyone who wants to reach his or her "peak performance." Coach Brown has contributed to the success of the football program at Nebraska for more than a decade.

Those who follow sports understand the need for athletes to possess certain character qualities in order to develop their skills and perform to their full potential. By using past examples from the Nebraska football program, we believe you will better understand how to reach your full potential.

Besides using the arena of Nebraska football to teach character qualities, we have also used these analogies and metaphors to teach important spiritual truths through parables. Jesus and other authors of the Bible often used them as well. There are many examples in the Bible that compare God's truths to raising crops and caring for sheep.

We believe the athletes or persons who truly reach their peak performance will develop themselves spiritually as well as emotionally, physically and mentally.

We wish you the best as you apply these principles to every area of your life, not just sports.

In His Grip,

Gordon Thiessen

CONTENTS

Peak Performance

INTRODUCTION 2

1. INTEGRITY   *Winners Work with Integrity*   4
2. GOALS   *Winners Work with Purpose*   6
3. PERSPECTIVE *Winners Keep a Positive Perspective* 8
4. DISCIPLINE   *Winners Sharpen their Skills*   10
5. EFFORT   *Winners Do More Than is Expected*   12
6. ATTITUDE   *Winners Have a Coachable Attitude*   14
7. PERSEVERANCE *Winners Never Quit*   16
8. PRIORITIES   *Winners Keep Priorities*   18
9. PREPARATION *Winners Prepare for Opportunity*   20

CROSS TRAINING RESOURCES 22
MISSION NEBRASKA 23

INTEGRITY

Winners Work with Integrity

PRINCIPLE NUMBER ONE

*Blessed are they who maintain justice,
who constantly do what is right. Psalm 106:3*

We live in a time when society's values have been turned upside-down. Not so long ago, integrity and character were considered important qualities. Now many have taken to the pursuit of personal pleasure and shortcuts to success.

A few years ago, Coach Ron Brown interviewed an athlete for his weekly "Husker Sports Report" who demonstrated integrity. In 1994, University of Texas kicker Phil Dawson had a super year in football. And as a result, he was named to *Playboy* magazine's 39th Annual Preseason All-American team. As a Christian, that was something he felt he could not accept. And he told the magazine so. When Dawson was asked to comment on his decision to decline an all-expense paid weekend at the Playboy mansion and the publicity of appearing in a national magazine, he said, "Many people respected my position, but some didn't understand. Taking *Playboy's* offer was not right for me with what I am trying to do with my life."

The dictionary defines integrity as "the state of being complete, unified." When people have integrity, their words and their deeds match up. It doesn't matter whom they are with or where they are. For kicker Phil Dawson it meant turning down an honor and trip that few athletes would decline because he had said he didn't support the values of *Playboy* magazine.

In other words, people with integrity do not have divided loyalties (that's duplicity), nor do they merely pretend to believe something (that's hypocrisy).

A person with integrity has established a system of values against which his or her life is judged. In the case of Phil Dawson, it was his Christian faith which was based on a system of biblical principles.

Here are a few more thoughts on integrity:

Image is what others think we are. Integrity is what we really are.

Integrity is not what we do as much as who we are.

Billy Graham said, "Integrity is the glue that holds our way of life together. We must constantly strive to keep our integrity intact."

Integrity lets us predetermine what we will be regardless of the circumstances or people involved.

There are at least two benefits to a person who lives a life of integrity: First, a person with integrity will have a clear conscience. Whenever you compromise your values in some area, it is likely you will feel guilt. Jim Wacker, a former TCU football coach, chose not to hide rule violations in his program when they were discovered. "The good thing is you live through it. It is over, and you feel good about it because you did what you believe is right. And if you do that, you can look at yourself in a mirror and feel good about yourself."

Second, a person with integrity develops a closer relationship with God. Psalm 15 in the Bible teaches that if we want to be close to God, then we must pursue a morally pure lifestyle. Pitching ace Orel Hershiser said he learned to say "sorry" to God by confessing sin as soon as he became aware of it. "I wouldn't even wait for my prayers at night. I would just confess at that moment."

Winners work with integrity, which results in a solid reputation, not just image.

Extra Points
1. How consistent are your words with your actions?
2. What helps you determine what you want to do and what you ought to do?

Action Point
Pick one area of your life in which you want to become more consistent.

GOALS

Winners Work with Purpose

PRINCIPLE NUMBER TWO

An intelligent man aims at wise actions, but a fool starts off in many directions. Proverbs 17:24

Tommie Frazier grabbed the face mask of a 300-pound offensive lineman who wasn't paying attention to him and screamed, "Shut up and listen! I'm the quarterback, and when I'm in the huddle, no one else talks!" For most football fans there would be nothing unusual about an All-American quarterback taking charge of his huddle; however, this was Tommie's freshman year, and the huge lineman was a senior.

Frazier's focus on accomplishing his goal was perhaps the characteristic that helped him become one of the best quarterbacks in college football. Because of his goal-oriented focus, the Huskers won two national championships.

Most coaches would agree with the following statements:

"Aim at nothing and you will probably hit it."

"If you don't know where you are going, you will probably end up somewhere else."

"If you fail to plan, you plan to fail."

Therefore, it is not surprising that most coaches spend a lot of time each season setting and working toward specific goals. Where are you going? How do you plan to get there? When setting goals, consider using the acronym S-A-M. When you set goals, make sure your goals are *Specific, Achievable,* and *Measurable.*

Specific: Many athletes set goals that are too general. Goals should be specific and achievable during a set time period. "I'm going to start lifting weights this season." (Wrong) "I'm going to bench press three days a week and do at least six sets." (Right)

Achievable: An unrealistic goal is just as bad as a mediocre one. If a goal is too far out of reach, it can lead to frustration. On the other hand, a goal needs to stretch you to your potential.

Measurable: You should always make sure to evaluate yourself before you set new goals. That way you can always be sure when you have reached your goals. "I'm going to spend more time running sprints." (Wrong) "I'm going to run three 200-meter sprints under 25 seconds after each practice." (Right)

While you may set goals in many areas of your life, there is one ultimate goal God has for you—to glorify Him in your life! The Bible teaches us to glorify God with our bodies. "...do you not know that your body is a temple of the Holy Spirit who is in you, whom you have from God, and that you are not your own? For you have been bought with a price; therefore, glorify God in your body" (1 Cor. 6:19-20).

The word "glorify" can mean to cause somebody to respect and have a good opinion of somebody else. When athletes are recognized for their outstanding achievements, they are often introduced with a highlight film. In a spiritual sense, we become God's highlight film for the world to view, as we glorify Him by our actions.

Winners work with a purpose in mind—make it your ultimate goal to glorify God so you can be all you can be!

Extra Points
1. What are your short-range goals for school, sports, work, etc.?
2. What are your long-range goals for school, sports, work, etc.?
3. What is the most important mission in your life?

Action Point
Apply the S-A-M method to at least one short-range goal.

PERSPECTIVE

Winners Keep a Positive Perspective

PRINCIPLE NUMBER THREE

Do all things without grumbling or arguing . . . and you will shine out like a light in a dark world. Philippians 2:14-15

The emotions surrounding Coach Tom Osborne's second consecutive national college football championship were mixed. His team had just finished dominating a great Florida team 62-24 in the Fiesta Bowl. "It was a terrible year, and it was a great year," the Nebraska head coach stated at a press conference following the game. "It was taxing. It was gratifying to work with a group of players with that focus and drive, and that is the saving, redeeming factor." Though this was considered by Osborne as perhaps his best team ever, the entire season was surrounded by controversy because of the misdeeds of a few players.

As it did so often in Osborne's coaching career, perspective helped to determine his behavior. He could have complained and given up any time during this difficult year at the helm of the Huskers. Instead, he kept a positive perspective that helped his team finish one of the greatest seasons in college football.

When talking about the importance of a proper perspective, Chuck Swindoll said, "The longer I live, the more I realize the impact of attitude on life. Attitude, to me, is more important than facts. It is more important than the past, than education, than money, than circumstances, than failures, than successes, than what other people think or say or do. It is more important than appearance, giftedness, or skill. It will make or break a company, a church, or a home. The remarkable thing is that we have a choice every day regarding the attitude we will embrace for that day. We cannot change the past. Nor can we change the fact that people will act a certain way. We also cannot change the inevitable. The only thing we can do is play on the one string we have, and that is our attitude. I am convinced that life is ten percent what happens to me and ninety percent how I react to it. And so it is with you—we are in charge of our attitudes."

Former Notre Dame coach Lou Holtz said, "Your talent determines what you can do. Your motivation determines how much you are willing to do. Your attitude determines how well you do it."

Whether you are an athlete or not, your thinking will show in your actions. "For as he thinks within himself, so he is" (Proverbs 23:7). This passage points out that the perspective a person has will surface in his or her actions. While many in the national media were puzzled by Coach Osborne's positive perspective in the midst of controversy, his behavior was no secret. When asked about how he copes with stress, Coach Osborne said, "I try to spend time each day in prayer or meditation. I also spend time in the Scriptures each day. My time spent in this fashion has been a real source of strength to me. In the book of Isaiah, it says that 'those who wait upon the Lord will renew their strength. They will mount up with wings like eagles. They will run and not grow weary, they will walk and not faint.' I know that God . . . provides the necessary strength to those who desire to serve Him."

The right perspective in life comes from a proper spiritual perspective that only comes from a relationship with Jesus Christ.

Winners keep a positive perspective by keeping Jesus Christ at the center of their lives!

Extra Points
1. What friend do you admire most?
2. What is the one thing that you admire most about this friend?
3. Does this quality describe an attitude, skill or appearance?

Action Point
Write down the right attitude you desire in one area of your life.

DISCIPLINE

Winners Sharpen Their Skills

PRINCIPLE NUMBER FOUR

If the ax is dull, and its edge unsharpened, more strength is needed, but skill will bring success. Eccl. 10:10

Few Nebraska football teams have had quarterback controversies during the past two decades. However, when Tommie Frazier was hurt and Brook Berringer stepped in to replace him, some fans began to worry about the team becoming weaker because of controversy once Tommie returned. However, their fears were misplaced, and the Nebraska football team became stronger because of the competition between the two quarterbacks.

Frazier was known as a better option quarterback, while Berringer was known for his passing ability. Because of the intense competition for the starting job at quarterback, both players were challenged to improve their skills. While Berringer sharpened his option game, Frazier greatly improved his accuracy and touch when throwing a football. Both players became true winners by sharpening their skills, which helped the Nebraska football team to another national championship.

The American Heritage Dictionary defines discipline as "training expected to produce a specific character or pattern of behavior, especially training that produces moral or mental improvement." There can be no doubt that both Berringer and Frazier produced outstanding results from their training.

Without motivation there can be no training which leads to better skills and positive results. What motivates you and others to be disciplined to achieve peak performance?

Many athletes are driven by circumstantial motivational factors such as personal recognition, anger, money, fear and revenge. Each of these forces may motivate us to take action, but all are inconsistent because they must rely on circumstances to be effective. For example, you might be motivated by revenge to give a great effort one week, but completely lack desire and intensity the following week against another opponent.

The peak performer relies on a far more consistent motivational force described in the Bible. It is the basic motivational force of love upon which God operates. "For God so loved the world, that he gave his only begotten Son, that whoever believes in him should not perish but have eternal life" (John 3:16).

The motivational force of love draws out the best in a person and remains consistent from day to day. For example: If basketball players have developed a lot of respect and affection for their coach, they will do practically anything they are asked to do out of their desire to please him.

You can express your love and respect toward God through your performance as well. The Apostle Paul wrote that, as a Christian, you can use your talents and abilities to express your appreciation toward God. "I urge you, therefore, brethren, by the mercies of God (because of how God demonstrated His love for you on the cross) to present your bodies (consciously commit your talents and abilities to God), a living and holy sacrifice (dead to your own interests and alive to God's interests) acceptable to God, which is your spiritual service of worship (the way you can express your love and respect to God)" (Romans 12:1).

Winners sharpen their skills consistently out of respect to the One who gave them the ability to perform at their best.

Extra Points
1. What motivates you to give your best effort?
2. Can you apply the Christian motivational force of love to your life? Why or why not?

Action Point
Consider how you can express your love and respect to God.

EFFORT

Winners Do More Than is Expected

PRINCIPLE NUMBER FIVE

If anybody forces you to go a mile with him, do more, go two miles with him. Matthew 5:41

Matt Davison's game-saving catch for Nebraska in 1997 was nothing less than miraculous! This "miracle catch" by freshman split end Matt Davison kept his team's hopes alive for a national championship.

With the Huskers trailing 38-31 and only 1:02 left in the fourth quarter, quarterback Scott Frost led the team down the field by expertly managing the clock. However, on Missouri's 12-yard line with only seven seconds remaining, Frost's pass to receiver Shevin Wiggins bounced off his chest as he was hit by a defensive player. As the ball flew away from Wiggins' body, his foot kicked it into the air, and Matt Davison made a diving catch that was ruled a touchdown.

The amazing offensive drive against Missouri that began with only 1:16 on the clock showed the Huskers' winning attitude to do more than is expected.

Many teams would have mentally given up with such a short time left in the game—especially an offense known more for its ability to run the football than pass it downfield. While there were many great plays during the Huskers' drive, nothing compared to the catch Davison made in the end zone to help his team win the game. He would later receive the ESPY Award for his effort. Many receivers might have stopped running when it looked like the play was over. Instead, Matt kept running to the ball and, when it squirted into the air, he was ready to receive it. A perfect example of doing more than some would expect and giving a complete effort on the play.

A few years ago, an article in *Sports Illustrated* asked the question: Does faith lower batting averages? At the time, several major leaguers were in hitting slumps, so a few reporters began to search for reasons. Some concluded that a person's faith could adversely affect their batting average.

Can you be a Christian and still be a hard-nosed competitor? Good question. The combination of Scott Frost and Matt Davison (both well-known believers) should answer this question with a resounding yes! Here are several other athletes responding to this question:

"Anybody that says I would be docile about losing, I'd challenge him to stand in front of home plate with the ball and try to block me and see if I have lost my intensity to play." —Gary Gaetti, major league baseball player

"If Jesus were on the field, He'd be pitching inside and breaking up double plays. He'd be high-fiving the other guys. That's what Christianity is supposed to be. Some players may lose their fire, but not because of the Lord." —Tim Burke, former major league pitcher

Convinced? Well, don't take their word for it—take God's. The Bible says, "Whatever you do, work at it with all your heart, as working for the Lord, not for men" (Colossians 3:23).

Did you catch the word "whatever"? This verse applies to every area of our life. The word "heartily" refers to giving our best effort every time we compete. No slacking off or taking it easy. And the motivation? For the Lord, not for your coaches, teammates or the fans.

Winners give their best effort at all times while doing more than others expect.

Extra Points
1. Do you agree with the comments made by Gaetti and Burke?
2. Former UCLA basketball coach John Wooden said, "The effort is what counts in everything." Do you agree? Why?
3. What kind of an athlete would Jesus Christ have been?

Action Point
Give nothing less than your best in everything you do.

ATTITUDE

Winners Have a Coachable Attitude

PRINCIPLE NUMBER SIX

For lack of advice plans go wrong, but with many counselors they are accomplished. Proverbs 15:22

Coach Tom Osborne had just finished warning his team during the halftime break to keep their mouths shut and not respond to the comments made by the other team. As the 1995 Huskers took the field against Miami in the national championship game, assistant coach Ron Brown credited much of their second half success to self-discipline and a willingness to heed Coach Osborne's advice.

"We knew as coaches that the 1995 Hurricane team was likely to push us into a trash-talking game. Coach Osborne knew we were better conditioned, so if we could keep from responding to their verbal taunts, we could win the game," Brown said.

Nebraska resisted the temptation to respond to the trash-talking Warren Sapp and his teammates during the second half. This coachable attitude helped lead the Cornhuskers to a victory that would become Coach Osborne's first national championship.

Winning in athletics requires a coachable spirit or attitude. Few athletes can ever reach their full potential without the advice or encouragement of someone else. All of us can use help from coaches to evaluate our performance, identify our potential and help us improve our skills.

During recent years, many of the greatest athletes in professional sports have begun hiring personal trainers to maximize their workouts. Whether it is an NBA player working with his trainer on increasing his free throw percentage or an NFL player working with his trainer on reducing his weight and improving his speed, coaching works!

While it is important to receive feedback and advice from a coach so we can sharpen our skills, so too must we allow ourselves to be coached spiritually by the word of God, along with the guidance of the Holy Spirit.

While every coach and athlete understands the importance of learning and applying the playbook, it is even more important to know God's playbook, the Bible, and apply its principles to life.

The written words of the Bible are "God-breathed"—that's what "inspired" in 2 Timothy 3:16 literally means.

How does the Bible coach us?
- Teaches us who God is
- Teaches us what God wants
- Teaches us what God offers

The Holy Spirit is the third person in the Trinity. He is God just as Jesus Christ is God. When Jesus told His disciples the Father would provide another "Helper, that He may be with you forever..." (John 14:16), He gave us the Holy Spirit.

How does the Holy Spirit coach us?
- Reveals to us who Jesus is
- Convicts us of sin
- Gives us understanding about God's Word
- Recalls God's Word to our mind
- Transforms us into Christ's spiritual and moral likeness

Winners transform their lives by remaining coachable while depending on God for what seems impossible or improbable.

Extra Points
1. How have you benefited from a coach's advice?
2. What are some benefits from reading and applying the Bible?

Action Point
Commit yourself to regularly reading the Bible each day.

PERSEVERANCE

Winners Never Quit

PRINCIPLE NUMBER SEVEN

*For if a righteous man falls seven times,
he rises again. Proverbs 24:16*

As a homegrown product of Nebraska with parents that competed for the University of Nebraska in football and track and field, it was assumed by most loyal Big Red fans that Scott Frost would follow in the footsteps of his parents. Instead, he attended Stanford and later transferred to Nebraska, which made some fans wonder about his commitment to the state.

As a starter during his junior season, when Nebraska lost to Arizona State, some fans put the blame on Frost. The team was coming off back-to-back national championships, and most fans had come to expect the impossible.

During his senior season, he was booed by some fans when the Huskers narrowly beat Central Florida 38-24. A week later, he finally redeemed himself in the eyes of many fans when the Huskers upset the No. 2 Washington Huskies. Frost recalled his thoughts prior to playing away from home in one of the loudest stadiums in college football. "Because there wasn't really anyone behind me, including a lot of my own fans, it was a tough time on me. It was a time when I could have given up, I could have been down on myself."

During the Washington game, Frost exploded with two rushing touchdowns in the first quarter to set the tone for the remainder of the contest. His 97 yards on the ground, 88 through the air, and two rushing touchdowns led to his being named the ABC-TV Chevrolet Player of the Game. Later that season the Huskers would claim their third national championship under Coach Osborne.

Perseverance. The word is the perfect description of Scott Frost.

Many athletes might have quit or given up when things got tough. However, Frost strengthened his resolve and became better rather than bitter.

Speaking about perseverance and persistence, former president Calvin Coolidge said, "Nothing in the world can take the place of persistence. Talent will not. Nothing is more common than unsuccessful men with talent. Genius will not; unrewarded genius is almost a proverb. Education will not; the world is full of educated derelicts. Persistence and determination alone are omnipotent."

Don Owens said, "Many people fail in life because they believe in the adage 'If you don't succeed, try something else.' But success eludes those who follow such advice. Virtually everyone has had dreams at one time or another, especially in youth. The dreams that have come true did so because people stuck to their ambitions. They refused to be discouraged. They never let disappointment get the upper hand. Challenges only spurred them on to great effort."

As a Christian, you don't need to gut it out on your own. It is a matter of relying on God for your strength. God can do amazing things through us by His power. Jesus said, "...apart from me you can do nothing" (John 15:5). The Apostle Paul said, "Now to him who is able to do immeasurably more than all we ask or imagine, according to his power that is at work within us" (Ephesians 3:20).

Remember, when you are faced with an impossible situation, stretch out your courage, hang tough and depend on Him. The Bible says, "Let us not get tired of doing what is right, for after a while we will reap a harvest of blessing, if we don't get discouraged and give up" (Galatians 6:9).

Winners rely on God for their ability to persevere. "I can do all things through Christ who gives me the strength" (Philippians 4:13).

Extra Points
1. In what ways is the spiritual life of a Christian more like a cross-country run than a sprint?
2. Which Bible character is a good example of perseverance?

Action Point
Rely on God's power to persist in every area of your life.

PRIORITIES

Winners Keep Priorities

PRINCIPLE NUMBER EIGHT

There is a right time and right way to do everything. Ecclesiastes 8:6

Who's No. 1? The 1997 season ended with two teams emerging undefeated and staking claims to the national championship title. Michigan entered the Rose Bowl as the top-ranked team but narrowly beat Washington State 21-16. However, the second-ranked Cornhuskers demolished No. 3 Tennessee 42-17 in the Orange Bowl.

Both teams felt they should be ranked No. 1. In fact, Husker signal caller Scott Frost spoke out following the impressive Orange Bowl victory by saying, "We feel like we're getting cheated. We've done everything it takes to win a national championship, and people just aren't responding to that. And all we can do is win our games and concentrate on what we have to do to be a good team."

Nebraska was awarded the Sears Trophy from the coaches' poll while Michigan earned the Associated Press Award for the national title. Since the two teams were unable to play each other, the only solution in most people's minds was to share the title. While a split national championship might seem fair in college football, it doesn't work when it comes to following Christ. Jesus said, "No one can serve two masters. Either he will hate the one and love the other, or he will be devoted to the one and despise the other. You cannot serve both God and money" (Matthew 6:24).

Jesus makes it clear; no split decisions when it comes to setting heavenly and earthly priorities. As the writer of Ecclesiastes said, there is a *right way* to do things. It is not just tough to serve two masters, it is impossible. The word (masters) refers to a slave owner. You see, it is not like being employed and working for several people. It is the idea of giving full-time service and being totally controlled and obligated to one person. To give anything less makes the master less than a master.

Besides doing things the right way, it is also important to do things at the *right time*. During the early '90s, the Cornhuskers struggled through several bowl appearances, so they began to evaluate their bowl preparation. They discovered that taking too much time away from the practice field prior to the year-end bowl game was hurting the timing of their finely-tuned option offense. Therefore, they increased the amount of time spent on the field during the break between the regular season and bowl game. While the turnaround in the Huskers' success in bowl games shouldn't be credited to only a change in priorities related to bowl preparation, it did contribute to their success.

Setting priorities is an act of the will. It is doing what needs to be done regardless of how you feel at the time. We live in a society where a lot of people are materialistic and serve money. Jesus tells us: He is the Master—not the games we play or the things we own. And it is not just money that can become our master. It might be power, prestige, or simply trying to please other people. Anything can push its way ahead of God on our priority list. Don't allow anything to squeeze out the Lord. Who's No. 1 in your life? If it is the world's values, it needs to change. One thing is for sure: God's not asking for your vote. He wants your life. A winner does the right things the *right way* at the *right time*.

Extra Points
1. What occupies most of your thoughts, time and efforts?
2. What will be valuable in heaven which isn't here?
3. If Jesus was not your master, what would be?

Action Point
Make the Lord No. 1 in every area of your life.

PREPARATION

Winners Prepare for Opportunity

PRINCIPLE NUMBER NINE

*The intelligent man is always open to new ideas—
in fact, he looks for them. Proverbs 18:15*

During the 1990s when the Cornhuskers managed to win three national championships, one guiding principle stands out. Those teams prepared for opportunity! Not in only one area but many. For example, during the early '90s, the defensive coaches shifted their alignment to a 4-3. For the football novice this might not seem like big deal, but this change helped the Huskers become one of the quickest and most dominating defenses of the decade. They also began to recruit players that were a better fit for this attacking style of defense.

Nebraska was also one of the first college football teams to start a unity council. The council allowed players to have a better channel of communication with the coaches and other players as well. This helped lead to greater team unity.

While it might have been easy for the Huskers to stay with ideas and programs that worked in past years, they continued to look for new opportunities in areas that other schools overlooked. They continued to improve their support for academics and even hired a person to oversee the nutritional needs of the athletes. They became leaner and quicker athletes due to the changes in weightlifting and nutrition.

During Coach Osborne's 25 years as the head football coach at Nebraska, most players will never forget one statement he made over and over. "You are either getting better, or you are getting worse. There is no staying the same." In sports, as in life, there is no staying the same. Winners prepare for opportunity by looking for new and better ways to do things.

There are four areas all athletes should prepare themselves for regularly. Physically, they must prepare their bodies to endure the rigors of competition. Mentally, they must prepare for the challenges they will face in competition. Emotionally, they must prepare for the moment they take the field or court. And most importantly, they must prepare spiritually. Legendary coach John Wooden once said, "Without proper conditioning in all areas, you will fall short of your potential."

While most athletes have some understanding of preparing for competition physically, mentally and emotionally, some are unsure of how to prepare spiritually. The following is Coach Ron Brown's personal account of how he prepared himself spiritually for the greatest opportunity of his life.

"I had heard all my life about Jesus Christ. I believed intellectually and conceptually in Him, but I had no relationship with Him. I was living my life on my own, calling my shots, making my own plans, pulling myself up the ladder of success by my own bootstraps until I came to an end of myself one day.

"All of these things that I was chasing began to leave me high and dry with an emptiness inside. Some call it a weakness, a crutch. I thank God that I finally realized I was too weak to control life and make it revolve around Ron Brown. Every person, including myself, was too weak to totally fulfill me. I thank God for the 'crutch' that He offered to me as a free gift—the cross of Jesus Christ.

"Jesus as God in the flesh came down to earth, lived a sinless life, changed hearts, healed the sick, performed miracles, was crucified on a cross for my sins, then was buried and rose from the grave. That day in 1979, I finally realized only Jesus could give me the love, purpose, and direction on earth as well as the home in heaven that I wanted so badly. It was then that I banked my life by faith that Jesus rose out of the grave, went back to heaven and is coming back one day to rule forever. That day I asked Jesus Christ into my heart, I decided to repent and turn from sinful life. Jesus will enter and rule the life of anyone who believes and trusts in Him as Savior and Lord for forgiveness of their sins. That day was the greatest day of my life. It was the day I truly became a winner by joining God's team. Are you prepared for the greatest opportunity of your life?"

CROSS TRAINING PUBLISHING

For spiritual encouragement and strength, join us at the Cross Training Publishing website @ www.crosstrainingpub.com. You will find valuable resource materials and other books written by Coach Ron Brown and Gordon Thiessen along with many other resources. You can request a free catalog at our website or call us @ 1-800-430-8588.

MISSION NEBRASKA

The seeds for Mission Nebraska were planted individually in the hearts of co-founders Ron Brown and Stan Parker years ago. God first opened their eyes to their need of a Savior, and then burdened their hearts with a passion to share their Savior with others. In July of 1997, God led them into conversations together that centered around their shared desire to see every individual in the entire state of Nebraska have an authentic opportunity to hear and respond to the good news of Jesus Christ. Their conversations and prayers culminated in the founding of this ministry in March of 1998.

Mission Nebraska is built upon three foundational truths. The first is the urgency of the gospel, illustrated by Jesus in Luke 15:1-7. The second is the comprehensiveness of the Great Commission and the possibility of its fulfillment in our generation, seen in Mark 16:15, 2 Peter 3:9 and Acts 19:8-10. The third is the necessity of a unified Body of Christ working together across the state, as prayed for by Jesus in John 17:21-23.

The purpose of Mission Nebraska is for Christ to be proclaimed across the entire state of Nebraska, giving every individual an authentic opportunity to hear and respond to the gospel.

The picture is to see the Body of Christ recapture her call to the Great Commission, then uniting around that call, be strengthened and work together for its fulfillment.

Ron and Stan write, "We believe God is desiring to bring about an evangelistic movement that sweeps across the entire state, and that He has raised up

Mission Nebraska as a catalyst to accelerate the rate of this movement on a local and state level.

"On the local level, our role is to facilitate the emergence of the local expression of the Movement. This will happen as we identify and begin relationships with those God is raising up to lead a unified Body of Christ into the harvest. Through these relationships, we will seek to resource these men and women as they discern and respond to God's unique plan for their area.

"On a state level, our role is to originate the vehicle that will allow the Movement to be expressed statewide. This will happen as we create the network that links the individual local expressions into a united whole, creating an unprecedented level of evangelistic synergy that positions the Body of Christ to fulfill God's vision for Nebraska!"

For more information, contact:

Mission Nebraska
PO Box 6225
Lincoln, NE 68506
Phone: 402-489-5018
Fax: 402-441-0631
Email: contact@MissionNebraska.org